Amazon Echo

The Simple User Guide How to Program Amazon Echo Fast (Alexa Skills Kit, Amazon Echo 2016, user manual, web services, Free books, Free Movie, Alexa Kit)

ANDREW JONES

CONTENTS

I think next books will also be interesting for you:

Amazon Echo

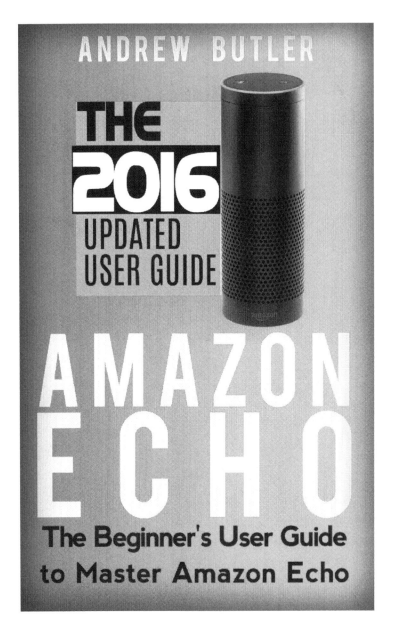

Amazon Echo

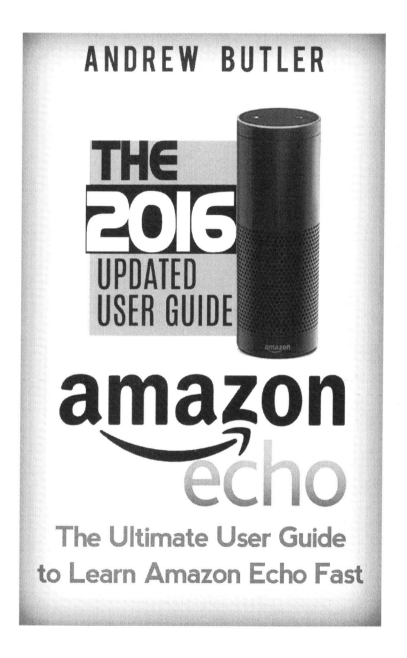

ANDREW BUTLER

THE 2016 UPDATED USER GUIDE

amazon echo

The Ultimate User Guide
to Learn Amazon Echo Fast

<u>Windows 10</u>

Alibaba

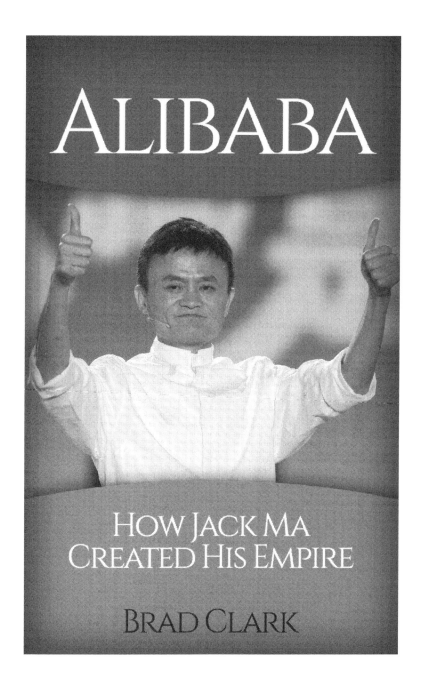

Amazon Prime and Kindle Lending Library

Introduction

In November 2015, Amazon launched its very own device compromising of both a revolutionary piece of hardware and an outstanding and ever developing software.

Entirely functional with the use your voice, there has been nothing like Amazon Echo on the market before now. Very much living in the present day, Echo relies on Wi-Fi and an app. But that's not all, the Echo is also super simple to set up. You'll see just how quick it is using chapter one.

To fight all rivals Amazon didn't stop there and released the Alexa Skills Kit for public use at no cost. Yes, that's right. It is free.

The Alexa Skills Kit allows developers all of skill levels from hobbyists to experts to create custom and smart home skills to personalize not only their own Echo, but share a new experience with other users. Day in, day out, new skills are being created and added to the Alexa cloud voice service and this is why Alexa is referred to as ever-developing software.

Before you get started with this guide and your Amazon Echo it is important to understand the difference in Echo and Alexa.

- Amazon Echo or Echo is the name of the voice command device itself.

- Alexa is the name of the cloud based voice service.

This simple guide will first teach you how to set up and use your Amazon Echo, before delving into the Alexa Skills Kit and sharing a step-by-step guide to building skills and creating a smart home.

Chapter 1 – Setting up your Amazon Echo

What's in the box?

Inside your shiny new Amazon Echo box you'll discover two essential items.

1. 1x Amazon Echo

2. 1x 21watt Power Adapter

Download the Alexa App

Free for Android, iOS, FireOS and supported web browsers the Alexa App has everything you need to control, use and manage your Echo device.

- For **Mobile**: Visit the app store on your mobile device and search 'Alexa App' and then choose the install option.
  Note: The compatible versions of mobile operating systems are:

Android 4.0 or higher, iOS 7.0 or higher and Fire OS 2.0 or higher.

- For **Desktop**: From Chrome, Firefox, Internet Explorer (10 or higher), Microsoft Edge or Safari, visit:
http://alexa.amazon.com
Note that your desktop must be Wi-Fi enabled to interact with your Echo device.

Turning on and off

Before you turn your Echo on choose a location to keep your Echo. You will need to be close to a power source but at least 8 inches (20cm) away from any walls or windows. Plug the power adapter into your Echo device, then into a plug socket and switch the power on. The light ring at the top of the cylinder will turn blue and then orange. On turning orange, Alexa will greet you.

Connect to Wi-Fi

Echo will not connect to mobile hotspots or Ad-hoc (peer to peer) networks.

1) Open the Alexa App > Open the left-hand-side navigation panel > Choose *Settings* from the options > Select your device > Choose *Set up a new device*.

2) On your Echo device press and hold the *Action* button for 5 seconds. This will change the Light Ring to orange whilst your device connects.

3) Return to the Alexa App - a list of Wi-Fi networks available for you to connect to will appear. If your Network does not appear choose *Rescan* or *Add a Network* from the bottom of the list.
Sometimes the Alexa App will also ask you to manually connect your mobile or desktop device to your Echo device through your mobile or desktop Wi-Fi settings.

4) Select your Wi-Fi network and enter your network password. If you are using a MAC you will need to add your Echo device to your router's approved list.

5) Select Connect > The Alexa app will display a message notifying you that your Echo is now connected to Wi-Fi

Changing your Wake Word

Echo's wake word is the word that allows you to communicate with Alexa.

By default Echo will respond to the wake work *Alexa* but this can be changed. There are two other wake words you can chose: *Echo* or *Amazon*.

To change your wake word > Open the Alexa App > Open the left-hand-side navigation panel > Select *Settings* > Choose your device> Scroll through the options> Select *Wake Word* > From the drop down menu chose your desired wake word > Select Save >The light ring will briefly flash orange.

Use Bluetooth to Pair Echo to Your Mobile Device

Echo has built in Bluetooth which means you can connect via Bluetooth to your mobile device.

- Firstly, turn Bluetooth '*On*' on your mobile device > Ensure your device is within range of Echo > Say "Pair" > Alexa will let you know that Echo is ready to pair.

- On your mobile device open the Bluetooth settings > Chose to pair with Echo > Alexa will notify you if the connection has been successful.

- To disconnect this Bluetooth connection say "Disconnect".

Once you have initially paired your mobile device with Echo you can reconnect as and when you want. To do this, simply turn on your Bluetooth   and   say   "Connect". Note: If your Echo is paired with more than one mobile device via Bluetooth, Echo will connect to the most recent pairing.

Getting to Know Your Echo

Get to grips with the functions that come on your Amazon Echo.

The light ring is a ring on top of the Echo which beams light in a variety of colors. Each color and light arrangement communicates the device and Alexa's status to you. Here is a table of Echo's common Light Ring codes for you.

Color or Light Arrangement Visible	What this means
Solid blue with spinning cyan lights	Echo is starting up
All lights off	Echo is active and ready for requests
Orange light spinning clockwise	Echo is connecting to your Wi-Fi network
Continuous oscillating violet light	An error occurred during Wi-Fi setup.
Solid red light	The microphones are off. (Press the microphone button to turn on the microphones.)

White light	You are adjusting Echo's volume level.

Other functions worth investigating include: Power LED, Action Button, Volume Ring and the Microphone Off Button.

Talking to Alexa

Start familiarizing yourself with common requests and questions that you can use anytime, here are a few:

- "Alexa, how far is it from here to New York City?"
- "Alexa, when is Mother's Day?"
- "Alexa, what is the capital of Brazil?"
- "Alexa, stop"
- "Alexa, cancel"
- "Alexa, louder"

Chapter 2 – Alexa Skills Kit

What is the Alexa Skills Kit?

Brought to you by Amazon, Alexa Skills Kit (ASK) is a collection of self-service API's. Whether you are an experience developer or an Echo enthusiast with ASK you can develop skills for Alexa. With a few short lines of code you can integrate existing services with Alexa or build entirely new ones, personal to you.

So, if you're an avid sailor and often require the tidal status for your sailing path; you can use a tidal report finder to create a new skill which will allow users to ask for the desired information. The voice request for this skill could be: "Alexa, ask Tidal Status for my local forecast."

ASK is free to download from: https://developer.amazon.com/ASK

There are two different types of skills that you can create through ASK; either a Custom Skill or a Smart Home Skill.

Understanding How Users Interact with Skills

Before you being to build your skills it is important to understand how Alexa and the user both work with skills.

As Alexa is built around voice recognition and voice command the interaction is different to a traditional app that uses graphic user interference. In simple terms, instead of tapping buttons and choosing options from drop down boxes, the user requests and responds with the device via voice.

Therefore, when a user speaks to an Alexa enabled device such as the Amazon Echo, the users speech is streamed to the Alexa cloud service. Alexa recognizes the speech, identifies what the user has requested, and sends a structured message to the specific skill that can fulfil the request/question and then Alexa delivers the result back to the user.

Every Alexa skill has an interaction model built within it. The interaction model begins with the wake word, followed by the user asking a question or making a request. Here is an example:

User: "Alexa, what's the weather?"

"Alexa"= the wake word "What's the weather? = the request

Alexa: "Right now in London, it is raining" = response

Interacting with a custom skill is similar to this but the user must include the identifying skill. Using the Sailors example, the interaction for this custom skill would be:

"Alexa, ask Tidal Status for my local forecast."

"Alexa"= the wake word

"Tidal Status" = the invocation name that tells Alexa the particular skill to interact with for the necessary data.

"Local forecast" = a phrase that is coded within Tidal Status and mapped to a specific intent supported by the skill.

In a similar way, a smart home skill will tell Alexa the skill to use in order to control a particular cloud-enabled device. E.g.:

User: "Alexa, turn on the bedroom lights"

"Alexa" = the wake word

"Bedroom lights" = the cloud enabled device which will have been programmed,

named and configured to turn on or off when referred to as "bedroom lights".

Chapter 3 – Custom Skills

Custom skills allow you to create a more interactive experience with Alexa. When you create your skill you will need to define the requests and intents that your custom skill can handle. An intent could be: ordering a pizza.

You will also need to define the words or phrases that users will say to invoke these intents. For instance this skills *utterances* could be; "Order a pizza".

A custom skill can handle any kind of request as long as you (the developer) provide the code to fulfil the request and supply the appropriate data which will allow the user to invoke the request.

A custom skill requires you to either code an AWS (Amazon Web Service) Lambda function or a web service of your own. AWS Lambda allows you to run code in the cloud without having to manage any servers, technically or financially. If you choose to create a custom skill through your own web service you will need to build and host your own HTTPS web service. This would incur additional processes and furthers costs, such a SSL certificate.

In order to build a custom skill you will need:

- An accessible internet end-point to host your cloud-based service.

- An AWS (Amazon Web Service) and developer portal account - this will allow you to host your skill as an AWS Lambda function. Or, a web service of your own.

- Basic understanding of Node.js, Java or Python

- An Alexa-enabled device for testing e.g. Amazon Echo, Echo Dot, Fire TV.

How to Build a Custom Skill

Step 1: Voice User Interface

To begin you will need to design a voice user interface. It is imperative that you do this before writing any code as this is the primary way that user with access and interact with your skill.

1. Firstly, create a flow diagram that displays how the user will interact with the skill. This needs to show the requests that users will make and ALL the possible outcomes. This will help to prevent problems later on.

2. Create your intent schema. Use a JSON structure to declare the set of intents that your skill can handle. Refer to the flow diagram to identify the intents your skill should expect.

3. Create a set of sample utterances. These are the phrases that users will say to access and interact with your skill.

Step Two: Set up the Skill

1. Create a name and invocation name for your new skill.

2. Register your new skill on the developer portal using the names you have created. Ensure that this is finalized before continuing.

Step Three: Create an AWS Lambda function.

- Create an AWS account if you do not already have one > Log into the AWS Management Console > Select AWS Lambda >In the top right hand corner define the *Region* by choosing from the drop down list > Choose *US East (N. Virginia)*.

Note: Lambda functions for Alexa must be hosted by this region.

- If you have previously created Lambda functions click *Create a Lambda Function*, but if you haven't click *Get Started Now*.

- If you want to begin by using sample code in Node.js or Python > Select one of these two blueprints:

  1) *alexa-skills-kit-color-expert*

  2) *alexa-skills-kit-color-expert-python*

  To find these blueprints quickly type *"Alexa"* into the filter box.

- Next, under heading *Event Source Type* ensure that *Alexa Skills Kit* is selected > Click *Next*

- Enter the name and description that you have come up with for your skill > Under *Runtime* choose the language that you want to use - this will be either Node.js, Python or Java. Once you have selected and saved this language for this function you cannot change it, therefore if you make a mistake you will have to delete this function and begin again.

Note: If you choose Java you will also need to upload your Java code in a zip file, but you will be prompted to do this.

- Under *Role* choose *Basic Execution Role* > Click *Next*

- Once you reach the *Review* page double check that the *Event Source* is set to *Alexa* > If all settings are accurate > Click *Create Function.*

Note: If you don't want to use AWS Lambda function for your skill you will need to create a web service and host it with a cloud provider.

Step 4: Write the Code for Your Skill

If you are using Lambda you will need to use Node.js, Java or Python. If you are using Node.js or Python you can:

- Write the code offline and copy and paste it in

- Write the code directly into the Lambda console editor

- Write the code offline and upload it using a zip file.

If you are using your own web service you can use any coding language you want to.

Note: Ensure that your code allows your skill to create a service that can both accept requests and send responses to the Alexa cloud service.

Step 5: Testing your Code

Once you have imported your code > Begin testing that your skill is viable.

You can do this simply by using the *Service Simulator* found in the developer portal.

Or you can use the AWS Lambda function from the developer. To do this:

Upload your code > Register the new skill and fill in the information required for your skill testing. > Next, select the *Lambda Amazon ARN* option and enter the Amazon Resource Number for your function > Set *Test* to *Enabled* > Test your skill.

To test your skill using a web service you can use the developer portal in a similar way but you will need to ensure that you deploy your web service to an internet-accessible end point and have the SSL certificate ready for testing.

Step 6: Submit Your Skill

Once you have finished testing you can submit your skill for certification, so that it becomes available to use by other Amazon customers. To do this ensure that you check over the submission checklist which can be found at:

https://developer.amazon.com/public/solutions/alexa/alexa-skills-kit/docs/alexa-skills-kit-submission-checklist

Make sure to update the data which explains what you skill is. This will be shown on the Alexa App. > Submit your skill for certification.

Step 7: Maintenance

Remember that even though you have published your skill it is always advisable to keep maintaining it. Enhance features, fix bugs, and improve the overall experience.

Chapter 4 – Smart Home Skills

A Smart Home Skill (SHS) enables you to create skills that control cloud-connected devices across your Wi-Fi network. For example; you could turn off your bedroom light without leaving the haven of your warm bed.

To build a SHS you can use the Smart Home Skill API. Although this will give you less control (as a developer) over the user's experience, it will simplify the development process as you won't need to create the voice user interface.

By using this process the Smart Home Skill API will define: the requests the skill can handle (known as *device directives)* and, the words that users say to make these requests.

For example a device directive could be turn on/turn off, and the words the user would say could be: "turn off the bedroom lights". As the developer of this SHS you would define how you skills will respond to a particular device directive. Following the same example, you would write the code that makes the bedroom light turn on and off. This is called a *skill adapter.*

To build a SHS you will need the following:

- An Amazon developer account. Visit: https://developer.amazon.com/ to registration is free.

- The cloud-enabled device that you want to control and use through Alexa i.e. light

- An AWS (Amazon Web Service) account - this will allow you to host your skill as an AWS Lambda function.

- Foundation knowledge of OAuth 2.0

- Basic understanding of Node.js, Java or Python

- An Alexa-enabled device for testing e.g. Amazon Echo, Echo Dot, Fire TV.

How to Build a Smart Home Skill

Step 1: Create a Skill

1. Open the Amazon Developer Portal and Login In > Click *Apps and Services* > Choose *Alexa* > Click *Get Started* > Choose *Add a New Skill* > This will open a page titled *Skill Information* > Select *Smart Home Skill API* > Enter the *Name* of your skill > Click *Save* > Copy the *Application Id* to your clipboard by right clicking and selecting *Copy* > Save this in a note on your desktop.

Step 2: Create a Lambda Function

1. Create an AWS account if you do not already have one > Log into the AWS Management Console > Select AWS Lambda >In the top right hand corner define the *Region* by choosing from the drop down list > Choose *US East (N. Virginia)*. Note: Lambda functions for Alexa must be hosted by this region.

2. Click *Create a Lambda function* > Select *alexa-smart-home-skill-adapter* from the blueprint page. Find this blueprint quickly by typing "Home" into the filter box.

3. Set the *Event Source Type* to *Alexa Smart Home* > Add an *Application Id* from the developer portal - this is copied to your clipboard >Click *Next*.

4. Enter *Name* and *Description* for your skill. > Select *Python 2.7* for the *Runtime* (You can also use Node.js or Java). > Check that *Edit Code Inline* is selected.

5. Enter the following code into the code editor.

```python
def lambda_handler(event, context):
    access_token = event['payload']['accessToken']

    if event['header']['namespace'] == 'Alexa.ConnectedHome.Discovery':
        return handleDiscovery(context, event)

    elif event['header']['namespace'] == 'Alexa.ConnectedHome.Control':
        return handleControl(context, event)

def handleDiscovery(context, event):
    payload = ''
    header = {
        "namespace": "Alexa.ConnectedHome.Discovery",
        "name": "DiscoverAppliancesResponse",
        "payloadVersion": "2"
    }

    if event['header']['name'] == 'DiscoverAppliancesRequest':
        payload = {
            "discoveredAppliances":[
                {
                    "applianceId":"device001",
                    "manufacturerName":"yourManufacturerName",
                    "modelName":"model 01",
                    "version":"your software version number here.",
                    "friendlyName":"Smart Home Virtual Device",
                    "friendlyDescription":"Virtual Device for the Sample Hello World Skill",
                    "isReachable":True,
                    "actions":[
                        "turnOn",
                        "turnOff"
                    ],
                    "additionalApplianceDetails":{
                        "extraDetail1":"optionalDetailForSkillAdapterToReferenceThisDevice",
                        "extraDetail2":"There can be multiple entries",
                        "extraDetail3":"but they should only be used for reference purposes.",
                        "extraDetail4":"This is not a suitable place to maintain current device state"
                    }
                }
            ]
        }

def handleControl(context, event):
    payload = ''
    device_id = event['payload']['appliance']['applianceId']
    message_id = event['header']['messageId']

    if event['header']['name'] == 'TurnOnRequest':
        payload = { }

    header = {
        "namespace":"Alexa.ConnectedHome.Control",
        "name":"TurnOnConfirmation",
        "payloadVersion":"2",
        "messageId": message_id
    }
```

Note: This code is only a starting point. This code determines the request type but the response is not fully implemented. Remember that you will need to handle every type of request that a user could make to your skill and provide all the necessary responses.

- Don't change the *Handler* default name from *lambda_function.lambda_handler*. A function handler is the main entry point for a Lambda function.
  The file name in the console will be *lambda_function* and the *lambda_handler* function will be the entry point.

- Next, select *Lambda_basice_execution* from the *Role options* > Leave all of the *Advanced Settings* as they are *(set to defaults)* > Click *Next*.

- Check that all the information displayed is correct > Click *Create Function.*

- When your function has been completed a summary page will be displayed. In the top right hand corner copy the Amazon Resource Name (ARN). You will need this to configure the smart home skill in the developer portal.

Step 3: Register Your Skill

1. Open the Amazon Developer Portal and Login In > Click *Apps and Services* > Choose *Alexa* > Select your skill from the list > Click through the *Interaction Model Tab* until you reach the page titled *Configuration* > Copy the ARN number from the Lambda function into the *Endpoint* field > Enable *Account Linking*. For this the following is required:

- Authorization URL

- Client ID

- Redirect URL

- Authorization Grant Type - for this ensure *Authorization Code Grant is* selected.

   For Authorization Grant Type you will need to supply the following:

   > Access Token URI ~ (The URL for the OAuth Server)

   > Client Secret ~ (This is so that the Alexa service can authenticate with the Access Token URI.)

   > Client Authentication Scheme ~ (Identifies the type of

authentication Alexa should use)

> Privacy Policy URL ~ (A URL for a page with your privacy policy. This link is displayed in the Alexa app and is required for smart home skills.)

2. Choose *Yes* to enable testing.

Step 4: Test Your Skill

To test your skill you will need to use an Alexa-enabled device.

1. Open the Lambda Console > Select your smart home skill > Click on *Event Source* Tab > Select *Alexa Smart Home* > Make sure *State* is enabled > Save > Close Lambda Console.

2. Open the Alexa App > Click *Skills* > Enter the name of your smart home skill > Search > *Enable* and *Account-link* your skill to the device cloud it is designed to work with.

3. Click the *Smart Home* tab on the home screen of the Alexa App > Choose *Your Devices* > Give Alexa commands using the utterances you have programmed your skill to support with device names you've set for the devices in your account linked device cloud.

4. Repeat Step 3 until you are satisfied.

Step 5: Submit Your Skill

1. Open the developer portal > Click on the *Alexa Section* > Choose *Get Started* > Select your smart home skill > Click *Next* until you reach *Publishing Information* > Fill in *Short Skill* and *Full Skill* descriptions. > Ensure *Category* is set to *Smart Home* > Add *Keywords* if you want to > Add small and large icons so long as they met the described guidelines > Add any testing instructions for the certification team > Click *Next* > Answer the questions about *Privacy and Compliance* > Click *Submit for Cerfication*.

Step 6: Maintenance

Remember that even though you have published your skill it is always advisable to keep maintaining it. Enhance features, fix bugs, and improve the overall experience.

Chapter 5 – Smart Home Devices (SHD)

By integrating Echo into your Smart Home, with Alexa's help you can 'hands free' your life in more ways than you can imagine.

Supported Devices

Since the launch of Amazon Echo in November 2015 the list of smart home devices that are compatible with Echo has kept increasing. Compatible devices range across lighting, fans, outlets, thermostats and some brands even supply starter kits so that you can begin building your shiny new Smart Home.

For a full and up-to-date list of all compatible devices visit: https://www.amazon.com/alexa/smarthome/devices

Connecting Alexa and a Smart Home Device

Before you can connect Alexa and a Smart Home Device you will need to:

1) Download the manufacturer's app that is dedicated to your smart home device.

2) Use the dedicated app to set up the smart home device so that it is connected to the same Wi-Fi network as your Amazon Echo.

3) Ensure that your smart home device is up to date with the most recent software updates.

To search for smart home skills available to your Echo Open the Alexa App > Select *Skills* > Choose *Refine* > Select *Smart Home Skills*.

Find the skill for your smart home device > Choose *Enable* > If required, sign in with your 3rd party information.

Return to the app home screen > Select *Discover Devices* or say "Discover my devices" - Alexa will should find your smart home device and connect.

If Alexa cannot find your smart home device check through these steps again. If Alexa still cannot find your device check the smart home devices companion app to ensure that it is connected to the same Wi-Fi network.

Removing a Smart Home Device

To remove a smart home device from your Alexa device Open the Alexa App > Open the left hand side navigation panel > Select *Smart Home* > Underneath the heading *Devices*, select *Forget* for each device you want to remove.

Chapter 6 – Extra Support for Using Amazon Echo and Alexa

Alexa Doesn't Understand You

If Alexa doesn't respond to your request or responds incorrectly to your request it could be for one of four reasons.

Firstly, check that Alexa has an active Wi-Fi connection. Alexa depends on an active Wi-Fi connection to access the cloud, answer your questions and process your requests.

Secondly, check that your Echo device is at least eight inches (23cm) away from any walls, windows and even other objects that could cause interference e.g. a microwave.

Thirdly, repeat your question or request making sure to annunciate properly. Speak naturally and clearly to Alexa. Minimize the background noise to ensure that Alexa can hear you.

Fourthly, be specific. Rephrase your question or make it less general. You can check what Alexa heard you say by visiting the *More* section on the Alexa App. This could help you to address an issue with your requests that is causing Alexa to misunderstand.

The Alexa App Won't Download

If the Alexa App will not download/install check first that you have the correct compatible operating system or computer web browser. You will need to have one of the following:

- iOS 7.0 or higher
- Android 4.0 or higher
- Fire OS 2.0 or higher
- Computer web browsers: - Chrome, Firefox, Internet Explorer (10+), Microsoft Edge or Safari.

Experiencing Problems Using the Alexa App

Problems Using a Mobile Device

For a mobile device you can have three options to resolve your issue. Begin with force closing the Alexa App and then reopening it to see if the problem persists. The second option is to restart your mobile device, again after restarting open the Alexa issue to see is the problem persists. The third and final option, if both the previous options don't resolve your issue is to uninstall and reinstall the Alexa App. For a step-by-step guide of how to do any of these three options for your mobile device see below.

For **Android**:

    1) Force close the app

On the Home Screen, choose *Settings* > Select *Apps* > Find the Alexa App in a list of installed apps on your device and select *Clear Data* > Wait for the app data to clear > Select *Force Stop*

Or

On the Home Screen, choose *Settings* > Select *Apps* > *Choose Manage Applications* > Find the Alexa App in a list of installed apps on your device and select *Clear Data* > Wait for the app data to clear > Select *Force Stop*

2) Restart your mobile device

Press and hold the Power button > Chose the option to *turn/switch off.* >Wait a few minutes. >Turn your device back on by pressing and holding the power button again.

3) Uninstall and reinstall the app

Open the app menu > Find the Alexa App in the list > Select *Uninstall.*

Once the app is uninstalled, visit Google Play and install the Alexa App again.

For **iOS** :

1) Force close the app

Press the home button twice until previews of all the open apps appears. Locate the Alexa App by swiping and swipe up to close it.

2) Restart your mobile device

Press and hold the sleep/wake button on your device until the power off slider appears at the top of the screen. > Press and drag the slider across the screen to turn the device off. > Wait a few minutes. > Turn your device back on by pressing and holding the sleep/wake button until the screen lights up and displays the company logo.

3) Uninstall and reinstall the app

If force closing the app and restarting your mobile device don't work then next you can try to uninstall and then reinstall the app to see if this rectifies the problem.

Start by pressing and holding the Alexa app icon on the home screen until it appears to shake. In the top right hand corner of the icon an X will appear, tap this. Once the app is uninstalled, visit the Apple App Store and install the Alexa App again.

For **FireOS:**

1) Force close the app

On the Home screen > Open *Quick Settings* by swiping down from the top of the screen > Select *Settings* or *More* > Choose *Apps & Games* or *Applications* > Select *Manage All Applications* or *Installed Applications* > Find Alexa App from a list of installed apps > Select *Clear Data* > Wait for the app data to clear > Choose *Force Stop.*

2) Restart your mobile device

Press and hold the Power button > Choose the option to turn off your device > Wait a few minutes > Press the Power button again to turn the device back on.

3) Uninstall and reinstall the App

Open the app menu > Select Alexa from a list of installed apps > Choose *Uninstall.*

Once the app is uninstalled, visit the Apps library and install the Alexa App again.

Problems Using a Web Browser

1) Reload/Refresh the Alexa web page

2) Clear the cache and cooking from your web browser by visiting *Settings* within the web browser.

3) Close the web browser, open it again and revisit the Alexa web page.

Resetting your Amazon Echo

At the base of your Echo device you will find a small *Reset* button. Use a paper clip to press and hold the *Reset* button. The Light Ring will begin a color sequence of orange > blue > then it will turn off and then return to orange.

This means that your Echo is now is Setup Mode. Open the Alexa App and Connect to Wi-Fi to resume using your Echo.

Conclusion

It is without doubt that Amazon have made a huge impact with the release of Amazon Echo. The technical overview of the device alone stands out from anything on the market. Built with 360° immersive sound, seven build in microphones, a responsive, sleek, stylish and practical app, the Amazon Echo provides everything you need for a hands free experience.

It doesn't stop there, by making the Alexa Skills Kit free for download, Amazon has opened up another dimension that easily could have remained closed. The ability to create and share skills with such ease gives Amazon Echo another mark above the rest. The possibilities seem endless.

As brands such as Samsung, Phillips, Haiku, WeMo and more continue to smart home devices onto the market, the ability to make day to day tasks entirely controlled by voice is a not just a nod to the future but a step over the threshold.

All in all, it is more than easy to say that Amazon Echo quite literally screams of modern day convenience.

Thank you for reading. I hope you enjoy it. I ask you to leave your honest feedback.

Made in the USA
Lexington, KY
02 August 2016